ANIMAL

Tyrannosaurus rex

DIARIES

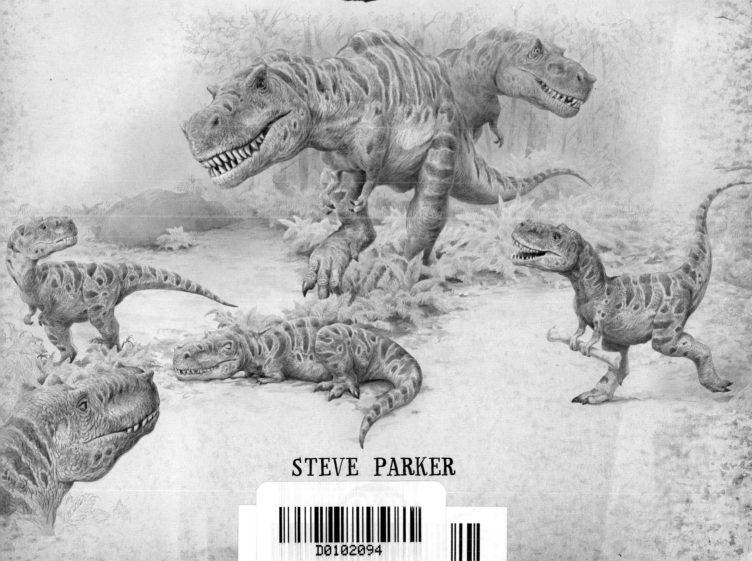

STEVE PARKER

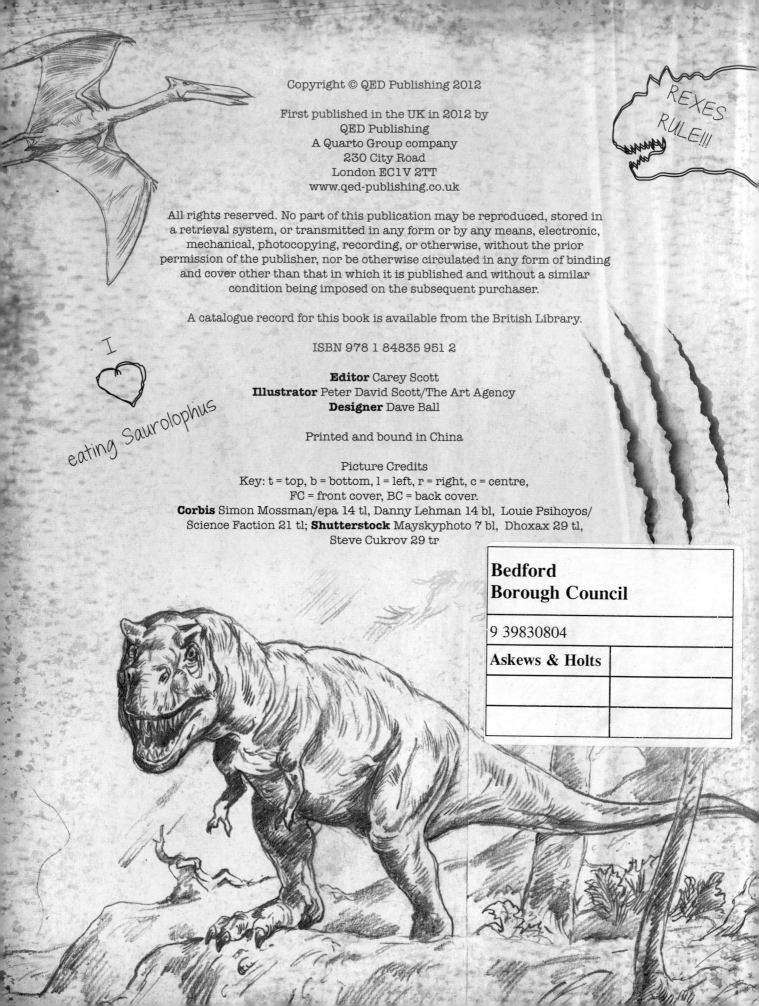

First published in the UK in 2012 by
QED Publishing
A Quarto Group company
230 City Road
London EC1V 2TT
www.qed-publishing.co.uk

ISBN 978 1 84835 951 2

Editor Carey Scott
Illustrator Peter David Scott/The Art Agency
Designer Dave Ball

Printed and bound in China

Picture Credits
Key: t = top, b = bottom, l = left, r = right, c = centre,
FC = front cover, BC = back cover.
Corbis Simon Mossman/epa 14 tl, Danny Lehman 14 bl, Louie Psihoyos/
Science Faction 21 tl; **Shutterstock** Mayskyphoto 7 bl, Dhoxax 29 tl,
Steve Cukrov 29 tr

REXES RULE!!!

I ♥ eating Saurolophus

Contents

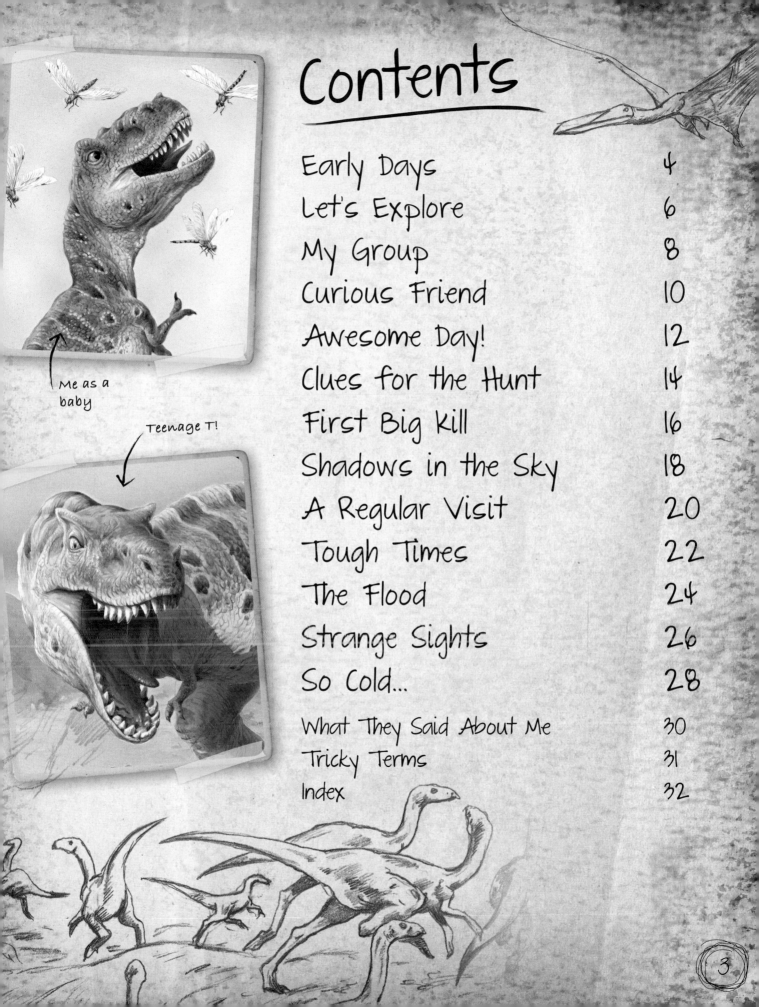

Me as a baby

Teenage T!

Early Days

I watched a nest of eggs hatch out this morning. There are now four new baby dinosaurs. It was dark and cramped in my egg, I remember. And as soon as the egg hatched I had to get used to the bright light. Luckily I was able to have a big stretch.

What happened when I hatched

It's dark in here

Bright light! Bright light!

Big feet! I could get squashed!

Wow, scary beast!

Here are some pieces of an old egg shell.

Tyrannosaurus
(Tie-ran-o-saw-rus)

Group Theropod dinosaurs

Adult length 12 metres

Height 4 metres

Weight 6 tonnes

Habitat Woods, forest, scrub

Food Other animals, including huge dinosaurs

Features Massive head and jaws, long teeth and claws, tiny arms

I'm feeling really hungry, so I'll try to snap up this dragonfly. It's not much to eat, but it will be good to practise my hunting skills.

Let's Explore

Every day I grow bigger and stronger. I'm also getting to know my area. There's the Three Hills, the Big River and Great Lake, the Vast Forest and the Endless Sea. I'm also spending more time alone, away from My Group. I've learned to sneak quietly, and to stop, listen and sniff often.

sharp pine needles taste terrible!

Dragonflies are too small for me now - I use up more energy chasing and eating them than their bodies contain! When you're a meat-eater, these details are very important.

Most of a dragonfly is hard wings, which have no nourishment.

The tastiest bits of a lizard are the muscles in its legs.

Every day, too, I'm getting better at hunting. There are so many animals to chase and taste! I caught a lizard and it bit me back. But I won, and it was delicious. Although two days later, I was hungry again!

Yesterday I reached the edge of the Endless Sea. I was thirsty, but the water tasted horrible. I had a rest and watched two birds - Hespers - catch their food.

Hespers' teeth are tiny but grip well.

Tiny, useless wings, a bit like my 'arms'!

I found a beehive hanging from a branch and could not resist a closer look. Buzzy bees cannot sting through my scales and skin, but one got me on my tongue. Ouch!

My Group

Every few days I come to the Clearing, where My Group (my family and other T-rexes) gather for important news. Of course we talk about food, like nearby herds of Green-Eaters. We also hear about dangers, such as fires and floods. I watch and listen, and learn how we T-rexes use our senses.

Our sense of smell is really good.

Like other dinosaurs, we have clawed feet and hands.

When we run, our tail balances our head and body. Neat!

T-rex eyes face forwards for a detailed view.

After we've all fed on the body of a dead Long-Neck, it's rest time. I'm learning about all my body parts and what they are for. So far the only use I've got for my 'arms' is... writing my diary.

Look at the Grown-Ups' huge teeth! At up to 23 centimetres long they're about the biggest of any dinosaur. They're long and strong, for ripping, tearing and crushing prey. Grrrr!

Old or broken teeth fall out, and new ones grow in their place.

Hey! I can pick up a Long-Neck bone with my 'arms'!

MY
WISH LIST

1. To be a Grown-Up tomorrow.

2. To eat a giant dead Long-Neck all by myself.

3. To have longer arms.

I can't wait to be a Grown-Up. It takes almost 20 years, which is a long time. Unlike some animals, the more dinosaurs eat, the faster we grow. So I'm always hungry!

Curious Friend

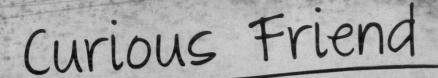

Yesterday I met a strange creature called Alpha. I didn't chase her because I was full up. Just as well - Alpha was much too quick for me. In a second she climbed a tree, out of reach. So I sat down below, and we had a chat about our lives and how we survive.

Alpha eats almost anything - even flowers!

Soft hairy fur keeps Alpha warm. What a great idea.

Alphadon
(Al-fa-don)

Group Marsupial mammals

Adult Length 30 centimetres

Height 10 centimetres

Weight 150 grammes

Habitat Woodlands

Food Bugs, worms, beetles, nuts, berries, seeds, flowers

Features Fur to keep warm, clawed feet for climbing

Alpha is so active! Even on the coldest days, she stays warm and races about. I can run in the hot sun, but when it goes cold, my muscles don't work. I have to lie down and rest.

Alpha is more cuddly than me! I've got really tough skin with hard scales. Alpha's skin has a covering of thin, soft hairs that she calls fur. It doesn't protect her much from bites and scratches, but she says the fur helps keep her warm.

I can stand up quite comfortably on my strong back legs.

Alpha seems to eat all the time!

Alpha stays up all night! When it's dark, she can still see, run around and feed. I can't, and anyway I get too cold. So ... yawn ... I'll finish the rest of my diary ... tomorrow ... ZZZZZ.

Awesome Day!

Today was soooo scary! My Group smelled some Three-Horns, and we followed them quietly. But just as we were about to attack, they smelled us, saw us, and charged. Panic! The Three-Horns were almost as big as our Grown-Ups. I was almost trampled to death. Awesome!

Triceratops
(Try-sair-a-tops)

Group Horned dinosaurs

Adult length 9 metres

Height 3 metres

Weight 10 tonnes

Habitat Scrubland, bush, wood

Food Low plants such as ferns and cycads

Features Long beak-like nose and eyebrow horns, big neck frill

Here are my pictures of the big fight. My drawings are getting quite good!

My trophy - a Three-Horn broke this on a tree. Now it's a Two-Horn, ha!

When Three-Horns find fresh plants, they're usually so hungry that they don't notice us. But this time the wind changed...

... and blew our scent towards them. At once they turned to face us, lowered heads and horns, and rushed in a ~~stampeed~~ stampede!

As the Three-Horns jabbed and stabbed, My Group scattered and ran. We all got back to the Clearing, but a couple of us were injured.

Clues for the Hunt

When I was little, I thought it was easy for T-rexes to find food. Now I know that it takes time and skill. I have to track my victim using all kinds of clues. Sometimes it takes hours. Even then the trail may fade, or the victim gets away. Hunting is really hard!

Droppings from long ago may get rock-hard. They're called ~~koprolite foskitts~~ coprolite fossils, and they don't smell, so they're no use to me.

Fresh droppings are brilliant! I smell them to work out whose they are.

Footprints in mud slowly turn into solid rock.

Footprints are another huge help. Their shape and size show me who made them. I sniff them too, to see if the scent is fresh or faded.

Scrape mark's size and
height = Horned One.

THINGS TO
REMEMBER

1. Always look, listen and sniff.

2. Attack young, old or sick
animals - others fight back.

3. Stay upwind
(remember when
I nearly died!)

Green-Eaters leave feeding
signs, like broken stems and
bitten leaves. Sometimes they
scratch trees and rocks with their
horns and claws, or they smear scent
marks. On each hunt I learn more, and
my skills improve.

Nibble marks like
this = Long-Neck.

Pooh! Scent smear
on this rock =
Beak-Mouth.

First Big Kill

Today was epic! It was the first time I've killed a big victim on my own. She was a young Beak-Mouth called Sauro. It took me half a day of tracking to get her. When I attacked, I was probably as scared as she was!

My brother also attacked - he killed a bigger Beak-Mouth.

Saurolophus
(Saw-rol-o-fus)

I followed Sauro past the Three Hills and through the Vast Forest. I could see she was getting tired. When she went out into the open, I suddenly charged!

Group Duck-billed dinosaurs

Adult length 12 metres

Height 4 metres

Weight Up to 4 tonnes

Habitat Woods, scrub, swamps

Food Plants, even tough leaves and seeds

Features Toothless beak-like front to the mouth, spike on head

My broken tooth - 20 centimetres long!

Sauro put up a good fight. She lashed with her tail and kicked. She tried to nip me with her mouth, which looks like a beak at its front. But I used my new tactic: I jumped forward, bit her hard, then quickly moved away.

I've got the strongest bite I know. It's even more powerful than Croc's.

My newest teeth worked really well – only one broke.

Sauro was badly wounded and bleeding, and soon she lost strength. Then it was safe for me to move in for the final kill. Now I've got a massive feast - enough to last for weeks. Yum!

Shadows in the Sky

I wish I could fly! But no dinosaurs can. When I go exploring, I often see creatures swooping overhead. There are two main kinds. One kind has feathers. They are birds, like Hesper and Ichthy.

Quetzy's kind can soar without flapping.

Here Quetzy's pecking meat off a dead body.

Quetzalcoatlus
(Cwet-zal-coat-lus)

Group Pterosaurs

Adult length 9 metres

Wingspan Up to 10 metres

Weight 200 kilogrammes

Habitat Plains, scrub

Food Small animals, dead prey

Features Toothless beak-like mouth, huge wings, long legs

The other kind of flier has wings of strange stretchy skin. The biggest one I know is Quetzy. His wings are as long as me! Quetzy can run on his clawed hands and feet as he hunts small animals. Or he flaps into the air and soars really high. He's so cool!

Ichthyornis
(Ick-thee-or-nis)

Group Birds

Length 24–30 centimetres

Wingspan Around 40 centimetres

Weight Less than 1 kilogramme

Habitat Seashores, open ocean

Food Fish, crabs, other small sea animals

Features Small teeth in beak, strong wings

Ichthy and her friends dive into the water to catch strange scaly creatures. I think they're called fish. These birds also make lots of squawking noises, which are very different from the hisses and roars that us dinos make.

Tiny teeth in the middle of the mouth grip slippery fish.

After diving for a fish feast, she dries out her feathers.

WHAT I DID TODAY

1. Finished off the dead body Quetzy was eating.

2. Paddled in the Great Lake.

3. Tried some fish. Yuck, too salty.

A Regular Visit

It's time to travel to the nesting colony again. Each year My Group goes there to feed on a huge group of Beak-Mouths, who are laying eggs and looking after their babies. It's a long way ~~their~~ there, but worth the journey. We can eat enough to last us for weeks.

I set off from the Clearing.

Tall Smoky roared and shook the ground.

Food on the go – if there's any meat on this dead dinosaur!

I trot past the Vast Forest, the Three Hills and the Big River, where I stop to cool off and have a drink. I've followed other T-rexes here before, and now I know the way by myself.

Here's a baby Beak-Mouth just hatching – killed and preserved by hot ash from Tall Smoky.

At the nesting colony, mothers make nests and lay their eggs. Unusually for dinosaurs, Beak-Mouths also bring food for their new babies. We gobble up the eggs and babies, and even some of the mothers.

It's a tricky scramble over Rock Bridge, with cliffs below.

The babies' nests are made of scooped mud and stones.

I stay well away from the Tumbling Falls.

Maiasaura
(Mah-ee-ah-sawr-uh)

Group Duck-billed dinosaurs

Adult length 9 metres

Height 2.5 metres

Weight 3.5 tonnes

Habitat Scrub, bush, woods, swamps

Food Leaves, berries and seeds

Features Looked after and fed their babies in the nest for about a year.

Tough Times

I can crunch up the smaller bones.

DROUGHT ENTERS 6TH MONTH – MANY DEAD

The Small Pond has shrunk so much, it could dry up next week.

The drought, which has been affecting huge areas of Our Land from Tall Smoky to the Endless Sea, looks set to continue. Weather-watchers predict at least one more month without rain. Trees in the Vast Forest have lost their leaves, and many ground plants have died. This means food is scarce for Green-Eaters. One Long-Neck said yesterday: "The herd has never seen anything like it. Our Leader, who is 80 years old, cannot remember a drought that lasted this long.

Some old and young have died of hunger and thirst." The Beak-Mouths have also suffered greatly. Even their food of tough pine needles is running out.

It's not bad news for everyone, however. As Green-Eaters perish, hunters such as T-rex get to feed on the dead bodies, and grow big and fat. A spokes-dinosaur for My Group of T-rexes stated: "We are sorry for those who are hungry and thirsty. But that's life – or rather, death."

The drought has brought us T-rexes together. There are so many dead bodies, we don't have to hunt on our own, or guard our kills from each other. There's meat everywhere. We can eat, rest and chat all day.

Deinosuchus
(Die-no-sue-kus)

Group Crocodiles

Adult length 11 metres

Height 1 metre

Weight 8 tonnes

Habitat Rivers, lakes, swamps, estuaries

Food Dinosaurs, fish, birds, turtles

Features Rounded rear teeth for crushing, big tail for swimming

We quickly tear the carcass to pieces.

Deino pulls the Mosa to deeper water to eat it.

I thought my bite was powerful, but Deino's is even stronger. He can tear tougher skin and crunch thicker bone than me. He's caught a mosasaur stranded in the shallows. The Mosa can swim but not walk. Deino can do both!

The Flood

The drought has ended at last. There's a huge storm and the Big River has overflowed. The flood is coming so fast that many animals can't escape. Some of them could drown. Great - easy meat for me! I'll hurry to higher ground for now, then come back when the water has gone.

I was friends with a baby Edmo for a few days. Then I found out that grown-up T-rexes hunt Edmos. I wouldn't want to eat an old friend!

Struth can easily escape the flood. She'd win any race - she's the fastest runner I know. She's got no teeth, but her strong beak has a powerful peck, and she can eat almost any kind of food - from leaves and seeds to bugs and dead bodies.

I just ignore Struth. She's too quick to catch and too thin to make a good meal.

Edmontosaurus
(Ed-mon-toe-saw-rus)

Group Duck-billed dinosaurs

Adult length 13 metres

Height 4 metres

Weight 4 tonnes

Habitat Forests and swamps

Food Plants, including hard twigs and conifer needles

Features Lots of wide, flat teeth for chewing. Wide, heavy tail

Struthiomimus
(Stroo-thee-owe-me-mus)

Group Theropod dinosaurs

Adult length 4.5 metres

Height 1.8 metres

Weight 150 kilogrammes

Habitat Scrub, bush, plains

Food Plants, bugs, lizards

Features Long, strong legs for fast running, beak-like mouth

Strange Sights

Today I saw two suns! The new one is a big, bright ball travelling fast across the sky. It's quickly getting bigger, and it stays in the sky all night as well as all day. But it might hit the ground soon. I wonder, will it cause any damage?

Stego's teeth are small, for nibbling soft plants.

Bone-Heads have thick, hard head-tops.

The Bone-Heads aren't bothered about the extra sun. They're too busy fighting. I'm not sure why. They snort, stamp and head-butt each other. I think they are battling to be chief of their group.

This extra sun will make it bright tonight!

They fight by knocking each other sideways.

I've just looked up again at the new sun and now it's even lower. The real sun dims as it sinks down and sets, but this new one's getting brighter. Random!

Stegoceras
(Steg-oss-er-us)

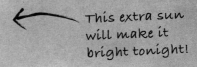

Group Bone-headed dinosaurs

Adult length 2 metres

Height 1.2 metres

Weight 50 kilograms

Habitat Woods, scrub, coastal areas

Food Soft plants

Features Thickened skull bone, like a crash-helmet

I'll leave the Bone-Heads to their contest. I know they're not afraid of T-rexes. If we try to catch them, they head-butt us too! They lower their hard heads, run fast and bash into our legs. Ouch!

So Cold...

I'm so cold, I can hardly ~~rite~~ write. After the extra sun went down, there was a huge crash, and the ground trembled. Ever since, the real sun has been hidden by dust clouds.

Plants withered and the Green-Eaters soon starved. We eat their bodies but there's no one left to hunt. Soon we'll be starving too.

Struth usually runs away, but there's nowhere left to run.

Three-Horns soon ran out of plants and got too cold to move.

I drew these animals last week. They seemed to be surviving the darkness and cold but I don't know why. Most are smaller than me, or they live in water.

Snakes are so slim, they can hide in holes and sleep there for months.

Crocodiles still have plenty of food - fish are surviving.

Lizards can eat almost any kind of food, not just meat or plants.

Mammals stay warm all the time, to search for food.

Birds can keep their bodies warm and fly away from danger.

Some animals are OK, like little Alpha, the birds and the bugs. But all the dinosaurs are dying. I'll just lie down for a while...

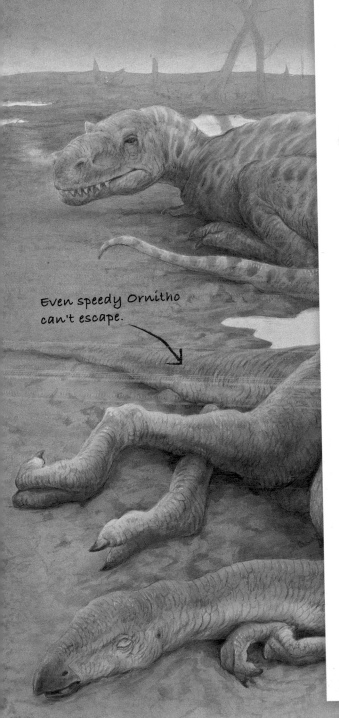

Even speedy Ornitho can't escape.

DINOSAURS LIVE!

About 65 million years ago a huge space rock, or meteorite, crashed into Earth. It threw up dust that blotted out the sun, and set off volcanoes, earthquakes and huge waves. For a long time, scientists believed that the dinosaurs died out, along with pterosaurs in the air, mosasaurs and similar water reptiles, and many other living things.

TOP LEFT: Parrots are just one of the 10,000 kinds of birds alive now.

TOP RIGHT: Seagulls live in much the same way as Ichthyornis did, during the Age of Dinosaurs.

But it now seems certain that some small, meat-eating dinosaurs evolved to grow feathers rather than scales. And in some of them, arms became wings. This is how birds began. But it does not mean that birds are no longer dinosaurs. Modern science says that they are members of the dinosaur group. So not all the dinosaurs died out. Some live on today – as birds.

What They Said About Me

M y diary describes what I thought of all the creatures I met. But what did they think about me? Let's find out...

Ichthyornis

Alphadon

> Like Quetzy says, it's great fun being a flier. But I spend hours cleaning my feathers. All T-rex does is scratch its scales occasionally.

> Imagine being too cold to move! It means you don't have to eat so much food, because you don't have to make heat energy from it. But I'd rather eat more and be warm-blooded.

> It's easy to scare off T-rexes. We just wave our horns, and our neck frills look so frightening. We're safe if we stay in our herds.

> I feel sorry for T-rex. It can't fly, only walk and run. I can do all three! I'd like to have T-Rex's long, sharp teeth. The problem is that teeth are too heavy for us fliers.

Quetzalcoatlus

Triceratops

Maiasaura

> I was never scared of that T-rex. I knew I could easily run away. T-rexes might have strong legs, but they're too short for real speed.

> The T-rexes always come and steal our babies. That's why we try so hard to get a nest in the middle of the colony. It's safer than being on the edge.

Struthiomimus

Tricky Terms

Age of the Dinosaurs The time between about 220 and 65 million years ago, when dinosaurs were the main large land animals.

Beak-Mouths Our T-rex's name for plant-eating dinosaurs called duckbills or hadrosaurs. Each had a beak-shaped front to the mouth, lots of chewing back teeth, strong front legs, powerful back legs and a muscular tail.

Bone-Heads Our T-rex's name for plant-eating dinosaurs called pachycephalosaurs. Each had very thick bone on the top of the skull, small teeth, little front legs, stronger back legs and a medium-length tail.

Cold-blooded A creature that cannot make warmth inside its body, and so is usually at the same temperature as its surroundings.

Coprolite A dropping (lump of dung) that has been buried by particles such as sand or mud, and gradually turned into rock, as a fossil.

Drought A long period, months or perhaps years, with no rain or other forms of water.

Green-Eaters Plant-eating dinosaurs, including the Long-Necks, Beak-Mouths and Three-Horns.

Hesperonis A large, flightless bird that lived in what is now North America during the Age of the Dinosaurs.

Long-Necks Our T-rex's name for dinosaurs called sauropods, mostly giant plant-eaters. Each had a small head, very long neck, wide body, four thick legs, and a very long tail.

Meteorite A large rock whizzing through space that crashes into planet Earth.

Mosasaur A large sea-living reptile with long sharp teeth and four legs shaped like flippers.

My Group Our diary-writer and his family and friends – a small group of T-rexes who hung out and occasionally hunted together.

Nesting colony An area where a group of animals gathers to breed, by making nests and laying their eggs in them.

Prey A creature that is caught and eaten by another, the hunter or predator.

Pterosaur A flying reptile, with front limbs shaped like wings made of very thin skin held out by long finger bones.

Reptile Usually a cold-blooded animal with an inner skeleton of bones. Most reptiles breathe air, have a covering of scales and breed by laying eggs. Most also have four limbs but some, like snakes, have none.

Three-Horns Our T-rex's name for plant-eating dinosaurs called ceratopsians. Each had sharp horns on the face, a wide neck frill, a wide body, four short legs and a small tail.

Stegoceras

> I like having a thick dome of bone on top of my head. It means I can head-butt almost anyone - rivals in my herd, Stegos, and even hunters like T-rex.

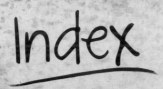

Index